The Concise Illustrated Bo
Butterflies

Michael Easterbrook

GALLERY BOOKS
An imprint of W. H. Smith Publishers Inc.
112 Madison Avenue
New York, New York 10016

First published in the United States of America
by GALLERY BOOKS
An imprint of W.H. Smith Publishers Inc.
112 Madison Avenue
New York, New York 10016

ISBN 0-8317-1692-4

Printed in Portugal

Right: A Viceroy butterfly covered in early
morning dew.

Acknowledgments
The photographs in this book were supplied by
the following agencies and photographers.
Michael Easterbrook: pages 14, 30, 44
Natural History Photographic Agency: James H.
Carmichael, front cover; Stephen Dalton, back
cover, 23.
Natural Science Photos:
S. Bharaj 33; Nigel Charles 20, 37, 38, 46; M.
Chinery 7; Stephen Davis 25; Richard Revels
10, 12, 13, 32, 34; P.H. Ward 11, 31, 40; P.H. &
S.L. Ward 16, 28, 41; Curtis E. Williams 36.
Tom Stack & Associates:
Nancy Adams 8; Christopher Crowley 17; John
Gerlach 4, 9, 19, 22, 24, 26, 42; Kerry I. Givens
35; Don & Esther Phillips 18, 39; Rod Planck 15;
Milton Rand 27, 45; D. Wilder 29.
All artworks supplied by Alan Male of Linden
Artists.

CONTENTS

INTRODUCTION

Butterflies are some of the most colourful creatures on Earth, and undoubtedly the most popular insects. They often stray into our parks and gardens, making a flower border even more beautiful by their presence. Unfortunately, this beauty is transient, as butterflies usually live for only a few weeks, or even days, though they may have lived for several months as caterpillars.

Their complex life cycle is also fascinating. Who can forget the wonder on learning, as a child, that a rather ugly, earth-bound caterpillar can turn into a beautiful flying creature? The process by which this incredible transformation occurs, inside the resting stage known as a pupa or chrysalis, is still incompletely understood, but involves complex chemical changes.

After hatching from the egg, the caterpillar becomes little more than an eating machine, with vast increases in size and weight. Its skin (cuticle) is unable to expand fast enough to accommodate this growth, so at intervals a moult occurs, in which the old skin is shed and the larva rapidly increases in size before the new skin hardens. There are often five or six stages (instars) between moults, before the fully-fed larva changes into a chrysalis.

When the butterfly first emerges from the chrysalis its wings are crumpled, and it has to pump blood through the veins to expand them. The lovely colours of the wings may be due to coloured pigments or to selective reflection and diffraction of light as it hits the tiny overlapping scales that make up the surface of the wing.

Butterflies can only feed on liquid food, such as flower nectar, and they do this via a specialized sucking tube, called a proboscis, which is rather like a drinking straw. When not in use this is held coiled beneath the head like a watch spring. To enable them to detect sources of food, and the correct foodplants for their larvae on which to lay their eggs, they have sense organs on their feet.

Unfortunately, in recent years, many butterflies have become reduced in range and numbers, and in some cases made extinct, often because of man's activities. The main cause of these reductions is loss of habitat containing suitable foodplants, as urban areas expand or land is farmed. To avert more losses, it is vital that we preserve suitable habitats and learn more about the requirements, often complex, of our butterflies.

★★★

The butterflies featured in this book vary greatly in size. This is not represented in the illustrations, so for the actual size reference should be made to the text.

Family: Papilionidae.

Habitat: Wooded and scrubby areas, mountain sides, canyons, meadows and arctic tundra in North America; wetland in Britain.

Distribution: Much of Canada south of Hudson Bay except extreme east; Alaska and much of western U.S.A. except coastal areas; Europe, including eastern England; North Africa.

Description: Large; wingspan 70–100mm ($2\frac{3}{4}$–4 in). Usually yellow with black areas and lines, and, on the hindwing, a band of large, shiny blue

spots, containing an orange-red spot near the inner margin. Hindwings have black tails. Undersides are paler, with less blue.

Life Cycle: Eggs are pale yellow and the young caterpillars are black with a white patch, resembling a bird dropping. When older they have black transverse bands containing orange spots on a green background, warning birds of their unpleasant taste. Two to three flights of butterflies occur in May–September in southern parts of their range in the U.S.A. and Europe, but further north one flight in June–July.

Larval Foodplants: Composites, including Dragon Wormwood and Arctic Sagebrush (*Artemisia* species), also umbellifers such as wild parsnips (*Heracleum*) in North America; Fennel (*Foeniculum*) and Milk Parsley (*Peucedanum*) in Europe.

General Remarks: The only true swallowtail butterfly with a circumpolar range, it is the only one to occur in Britain, where it is now confined to the Norfolk Broads. It has a powerful gliding flight, but stops to feed on flowers.

OLD WORLD SWALLOWTAIL (U.S.A.); SWALLOWTAIL (U.K.)

Papilio machaon

TIGER SWALLOWTAIL

Papilio glaucus

Family: Papilionidae.
Habitat: Deciduous woods, orchards, parks and gardens.
Distribution: Much of U.S.A. and Canada, and into Alaska, also Mexico.
Description: Large; wingspan 80–140mm ($3\frac{1}{4}$–$5\frac{1}{2}$ in). Uppersides usually yellow with black stripes and margins, though in eastern U.S.A. some females are almost completely dark brown (thereby mimicking distasteful Pipevine Swallowtails). Hindwings have patches of orange-red, yellow and blue near the rear margins and long, curved tails. Undersides are similar, but paler yellow and with a row of orange spots on rear of hindwing.
Life Cycle: Greenish-yellow eggs are laid singly on leaves. Caterpillars are green with two orange spots with black centres on swollen part of body behind the head, and rows of small blue spots. When not feeding they rest on a silk mat on top of a leaf. Several generations of butterflies are seen in the south, flying March–September, but number of generations and length of flight period decrease going north, to only one flight, in June–July, in the far north.
Larval Foodplants: Many trees and shrubs, including cherries (*Prunus*), willows (*Salix*), birches (*Betula*), and ashes (*Fraxinus*).
General Remarks: A spectacular sight because of their large size and strikingly beautiful tiger-stripe coloration, Tiger Swallowtails may be seen feeding at flowers, carrion and mud puddles, even in the centre of cities.

Family: Papilionidae.
Habitat: Open woodlands, meadows, fields, orchards, gardens and roadsides.
Distribution: Commonest in southeastern U.S.A., but is seen northward to southern Ontario and westward to Arizona and California. Also in Mexico.
Description: Large; wingspan 70–102mm ($2\frac{3}{4}$–4 in). Uppersides mainly dark grey-black, but with a lovely iridescent blue-green sheen, most noticeable on the hindwings. Females are less colourful than males. Hindwings have fairly short tails and some

cream spots. The underside of the hindwing has a series of large orange spots on a blue background. The remainder of the undersides is dark grey.

Life Cycle: Reddish-brown eggs are laid in clusters of 1 to 20 on the underside of leaves, and the young caterpillars stay together. Mature larvae are dark purplish-brown with rows of red and black projections, the two longest filaments arising just behind the head. Hibernates as a pupa. Several generations of butterflies fly at various times between January and October, depending on latitude.

Larval Foodplants: Pipevines and snakeroots (*Aristolochia* species), Wild Ginger (*Asarum*).

General Remarks: Pipevine Swallowtails are attracted to flowers, especially pink and purple ones. They migrate over long distances. The foodplants that the caterpillars eat contain chemicals that are poisonous to vertebrates. These substances are passed on to the butterflies and predators learn to avoid them. To take advantage of this, several other butterflies mimic their appearance.

PIPEVINE OR BLUE SWALLOWTAIL

Battus philenor

GIANT SWALLOWTAIL

Papilio cresphontes

Family: Papilionidae.

Habitat: Woodland glades and citrus groves, open fields and gardens.

Distribution: Much of the eastern half of the U.S.A., sometimes straying into midwestern districts and northern areas, rarely to Quebec.

Description: One of the largest North American butterflies, wingspan 100–138mm (4–5½ in). Uppersides are very striking with broad bands of bright yellow blotches running diagonally across the forewings to the tips, another line from top to bottom of each forewing, and one across each hindwing. The background is a contrasting dark brownish-black. Each hindwing has a dark, spoon-shaped tail, with yellow blob. There is an orange and blue spot showing on both sides of the hindwing, the rest of the undersides being pale lemon with black patterning.

Life Cycle: Light green eggs are laid singly on leaves and twigs. The caterpillar mimics a bird dropping, being mottled brown with cream markings. Behind the head is a long, forked, orange-red organ, called an osmeterium. This emits a foul smell, probably to deter predators. The butterflies may be seen throughout the year in the extreme south, May–September further north.

Larval Foodplants: Various citrus trees, Prickly Ash (*Zanthoxylum*), and some related plants.

General Remarks: Commonest in south-east U.S.A., and sometimes a pest in citrus orchards, where it caterpillars are called 'Orange Dogs'. Likes to visit flowers such as *Lantana* and orange blossoms.

Family: Nymphalidae.
Habitat: Woodlands and more open country, including parks and gardens.
Distribution: Throughout North America from subtropics to edge of arctic tundra. Almost everywhere in Europe except southern Spain, but only a very rare visitor to Britain.
Description: Quite large, wingspan 73–86mm ($2\frac{7}{8}$–$3\frac{3}{8}$ in). Has distinctive velvety chocolate-brown upper-

wings, bordered by blue spots and broad cream margins. The dark undersides give good camouflage on tree bark.
Life Cycle: Whitish eggs are laid in rings around the tips of twigs and the caterpillars stay together throughout their lives, feeding on leaves. The larvae are black, with many tiny white dots, a row of red spots and rows of long black branching spines. The butterflies hibernate, emerging in spring, often when there is still snow on the ground. They may be seen until late August in southern parts of the range, but the flight period is shorter in the north.
Larval Foodplants: Many trees, such as sallows and willows (*Salix* species), birches (*Betula*), elms (*Ulmus*) and poplars (*Populus*).
General Remarks: The common name of Mourning Cloak arises from the resemblance of the wings to a dark cloak with white trimming, while its name in Britain is the result of an early record in Camberwell, then a rural suburb of London, in 1748. The butterflies may be seen feeding on flowers, fruit and tree sap.

MOURNING CLOAK (U.S.A.); CAMBERWELL BEAUTY (U.K.)

Nymphalis antiopa

PAINTED LADY

Cynthia cardui

Family: Nymphalidae.

Habitat: Found almost anywhere, though particularly in fields, open ground, and gardens, even in areas at over 2,000m above sea level.

Distribution: Almost worldwide, except parts of South America, making it the most widely-distributed butterfly.

Description: Wingspan 64–70mm ($2\frac{1}{2}$–$2\frac{3}{4}$ in). Uppersides of wings are tawny orange, varying to salmon pink, with black markings and white spots. Undersides are pale grey.

Life Cycle: Eggs are green and the caterpillar constructs a tent from leaves held together by silk, in which to feed. Full-grown caterpillars are black and shiny, with a broken stripe of bright yellow down each side. The number of generations in a year varies according to the latitude, but in many areas Painted Ladies may be seen between April and October. They overwinter as adults, but are unable to survive in northern areas, such as Britain.

Larval Foodplants: Thistles (species of *Cirsium* and *Carduus*), Burdock (*Arctium*) and many other herbaceous plants, particularly composites.

General Remarks: Painted Ladies are well-known for their migrations, which sometimes involve large numbers of butterflies, travelling distances of thousands of kilometres in some instances. In North America they migrate from the southern states up as far as the Arctic, and there are similar northward movements from North Africa and southern Europe to northern Europe, including Britain.

Family: Nymphalidae.

Habitat: Woods, waste ground, gardens and orchards.

Distribution: Throughout Europe except northern Scandinavia and across temperate Asia to Japan. Widespread and often common in Britain.

Description: Wingspan 63–69mm ($2\frac{1}{2}$–$2\frac{3}{4}$ in). One of the loveliest of European butterflies, its distinctive 'eye-spots' resemble those on a peacock's tail. Eye-spots have red, yellow

and blue areas on the upperside of the forewings, while on the hindwings the blue centres are surrounded by black and white, all on a rich, velvety, brownish-red background. Undersides are a dark grey-black.

Life Cycle: Olive-green eggs give rise to caterpillars which are velvety black with white spots and glossy black spines when full-grown. They feed in June and July, producing butterflies that feed on a variety of flowers from July until the autumn, when they seek shelter for the winter, flying again in spring.

Larval Foodplants: Nettle (*Urtica dioica*).

General Remarks: When a Peacock butterfly is at rest on a dark background with wings closed, it is very difficult to spot. However, if disturbed, it will suddenly open its wings, flashing its colourful eye-spots. This deters many enemies, such as birds. In southern Britain, resident populations are probably reinforced by immigrants from continental Europe in some years.

PEACOCK

Inachis io

SMALL TORTOISESHELL

Aglais urticae

Family: Nymphalidae.

Habitat: Occurs over many types of open ground, including gardens, hedgerows, and woodland edges.

Distribution: Throughout Europe and across Siberia to Japan. A very familiar butterfly in Britain, where it is often abundant.

Description: Wingspan 50–56mm (2–2$\frac{1}{2}$ in). Uppersides of the wings are reddish orange, marked with yellow patches and black spots. An edging of blue crescents on the wing margins provides even more colour. In contrast, undersides are sombre, making the butterfly inconspicuous when its wings are closed.

Life Cycle: Small Tortoiseshells are on the wing on warm days in spring, after hibernating, often in sheds and garages. Green eggs are laid in large batches and the caterpillars feed in colonies until fully-grown, gradually reducing the foodplant to a skeleton. Caterpillars are yellowish, covered with black speckles and hairs. Chrysalis often has shiny gold areas on its grey background. The next generation of butterflies usually appears in June and early July, and in some areas there is another generation in August in warm years.

Larval Foodplants: Nettle (*Urtica dioica*).

General Remarks: Often seen in gardens, feeding on flowers such as *Buddleia*, *Sedum spectabile*, and Michaelmas Daisies (*Aster novi-belgii*). In North America, species such as the Compton or Comma Tortoiseshell, Western Tortoiseshell, and Milbert's Tortoiseshell are similar in appearance and life cycle.

Family: Nymphalidae.
Habitat: Woodlands and suburbs.
Distribution: Most of U.S.A. east of the Rockies, south-east Canada, and Mexico.
Description: Wingspan 60–67mm ($2\frac{3}{8}$–$2\frac{5}{8}$ in). Gets its name from the curved silvery line with dot beneath on underside of hindwing. Rest of undersides are brown, sometimes with purple sheen. Uppersides are tawny orange with black blotches and dark, purplish margins. Forewing tips

have hooked shape, and margins of wings have an irregular outline, with short tails on hindwings.
Life Cycle: Pale green eggs are laid singly or in small stacks on leaf undersides. Caterpillars are black with yellowish lines and many orange branching spines. The brown chrysalis has silver or gold spots. There are two broods of butterflies in the north, flying June–July and late August, and three to four in the May–September period in the south. Late summer butterflies hibernate until spring.
Larval Foodplants: Elms (*Ulmus*), hackberries (*Celtis*), Hop (*Humulus lupulus*), and nettles (*Urtica dioica*).
General Remarks: Question Marks are rarely seen on flowers, preferring tree sap, mud, carrion and overripe fruit, which can make them 'drunk'. They resemble dead leaves when resting with wings closed, but are strong, fast fliers, common over most of their range. Several similar-looking butterflies, including the several North American and one European species of Comma butterflies, have more indented wings and a comma-shaped silvery mark with no dot.

QUESTION MARK

Polygonia interrogationis

RED ADMIRAL

Vanessa atalanta

Family: Nymphalidae.

Habitat: Woodlands, orchards and gardens.

Distribution: Throughout North America from subtropics to Arctic tundra. Throughout Europe and eastwards to China and Japan, also North Africa. A regular and common visitor to Britain, breeding there but not surviving the winter.

Description: Wingspan 67–72mm ($2\frac{1}{2}$–3 in). Uppersides have striking coloration of scarlet bands and splashes of white, contrasting with the velvety black background. Forewings have delicate tracing of blue along the outer margin. Colours of undersides are much duller.

Life Cycle: Eggs are green, laid singly on leaves. Caterpillars vary in colour from greyish to dark brown or black, with spines, and sometimes yellow markings. They feed inside a 'tent' of leaves webbed together with silk. Number of generations depends on latitude, with up to four in southern parts of U.S.A. and Europe, where butterflies fly throughout the year, but usually two further north, May–October. Overwinters as butterfly, where not too cold.

Larval Foodplants: Nettle (*Urtica dioica*), Hop (*Humulus lupulus*) and, in U.S.A., some other plants in family Urticaceae.

General Remarks: Red Admirals sometimes undertake mass migrations, spreading northwards from southern U.S.A. into the northern States and Canada, and from southern Europe into northern countries, including Britain. Red Admirals feed on many flowers, including garden varieties, such as *Buddleia*. They love overripe fruit, such as plums and pears, sometimes becoming intoxicated, and so easily approached.

Family: Nymphalidae.

Habitat: Moist meadows and prairie, stream sides, open spaces, roadsides.

Distribution: Much of eastern and central U.S.A., and into southern Canada, also Mexico.

Description: Wingspan 25–40mm ($1-1\frac{1}{2}$ in). Uppersides are mostly an attractive tawny orange, and on this is black patterning. Undersides are yellowish, with less prominent markings.

Life Cycle: Pale green eggs are laid in clusters of 20–300 on the undersides of leaves. The caterpillars stay together when young. Full-grown caterpillars are chocolate brown with black and cream bands and many branching spines. Third stage larvae hibernate. There are many generations of butterflies in southern Texas and Florida, flying for most of the year; further north there are fewer broods and a shorter flight period, for example May–September in New York and Colorado.

Larval Foodplants: Asters (*Aster* species).

General Remarks: The Pearl Crescent is one of the commonest butterflies in the U.S.A., and is abundant over much of its range. It may be seen fluttering just above grassland, feeding at flowers such as asters (*Aster*), fleabanes and thistles (*Cirsium* and *Carduus*), or drinking at puddles. Males occupy distinct territories and dart out from their perches to investigate any intruder, be it butterfly or human. There are several similar-looking species of Crescent butterflies in the U.S.A. Their name comes from the pale crescent on the outer margin of the hindwing underside.

PEARL CRESCENT

Phyciodes tharos

BUCKEYE

Precis coenia

Family: Nymphalidae.

Habitat: Open places such as road-sides, embankments, fields, meadows and coastal areas.

Distribution: Resident in southern U.S.A. and spreads northwards during the year to most other states and southern Canada.

Description: Wingspan 51–63mm ($2-2\frac{1}{2}$ in). They vary highly in appearance but are usually tawny to dark brown with two bright orange blotches plus a yellow band on each forewing, and an orange band on rear of hindwing. Their most striking features are the lovely eyespots, which have iridescent lilac and blue centres and yellow and black rims. There are two spots on each wing, the largest on the hindwing. One forewing eyespot is visible on the mainly grey-brown undersides.

Life Cycle: Dark green eggs are laid singly on leaves or buds and caterpillars are blackish, with rows of cream spots and many black branching spines. Larvae overwinter, but can only survive in the south. Butterflies have many broods and occur throughout the year in the extreme south of the U.S.A., but further north are seen later in the year.

Larval Foodplants: Many, including plantains (*Plantago*), toadflaxes (*Linaria*), *Gerardia* and stonecrops (*Sedum*).

General Remarks: Buckeyes are common and widespread, especially in the south. They sometimes migrate in large numbers, with a southward movement along the east coast in autumn. They have a rapid flight, but stop to visit flowers or mud puddles, or to bask on bare ground.

Family: Nymphalidae.
Habitat: Woodland areas.
Distribution: Eastern states of U.S.A. and much of Canada, also into Alaska.
Description: Wingspan 70–80mm ($2\frac{3}{4}$–$3\frac{1}{8}$ in). Appearance differs completely in different parts of its range. In Canada and north-east U.S.A. there is a white band across both wings above and below, with most of the upper-sides black. In the south the white bands are absent, and there is much more blue-green iridescence on the wings, especially the hindwings. There are spots on the underside of the wings, orange in the south, brick-red in the north.

Life Cycle: Greyish-green eggs produce caterpillars that are brown or green, with a cream patch on the back and long dark horns on a hump behind the head. Butterflies fly from spring to autumn in the south, with several broods, and June–September or shorter further north.

Larval Foodplants: Willows (*Salix*), poplars and aspens (*Populus*), and birches (*Betula*).

General Remarks: It has now been shown that the two colour forms, which used to be regarded as two different butterflies, are subspecies of the same species. They feed on flowers, aphid honeydew, fruit, animal droppings and carrion, and groups may be seen on mud. Other Admiral butterflies in U.S.A. have a rather similar appearance, as does the British White Admiral, a totally different species.

WHITE ADMIRAL or RED-SPOTTED PURPLE

Limenitis arthemis

PURPLE EMPEROR

Apatura iris

Family: Nymphalidae.

Habitat: Woodland with oaks and sallows.

Distribution: In Britain restricted to a few areas in central southern England. Range extends from Central Europe eastwards across temperate Asia to Japan.

Description: Large; wingspan 75–84mm (3–3⅜ in). Males are smaller than females but have spectacular colouring, with wings shining a brilliant iridescent purple when light catches them at the right angle. At other times their colouring resembles the dusky brown of the females. Both sexes have broken white bands across the forewing and a solid white band across the hindwing, which also has a black spot with orange halo. Undersides are grey-brown with white bands and a black spot surrounded by orange on the forewing.

Life Cycle: Butterflies fly in July and August. Females lay glossy green eggs which produce green, slug-like caterpillars, which have yellow diagonal stripes on the sides and two horns on the head. They feed at night and hibernate when small.

Larval Foodplants: Sallows (*Salix*).

General Remarks: One of the most beautiful of British butterflies but difficult to spot, often flying around the tops of tall trees; the same ones often used year after year. They usually feed on aphid honeydew in the tree canopy, but males may descend to drink at puddles, sap, animal droppings or even carrion, behaviour which somehow seems inappropriate for a butterfly of such regal appearance.

Family: Nymphalidae.
Habitat: Clearings in woods, and tree groves around streams and rivers.
Distribution: Eastern half of U.S.A., also Arizona and Mexico.
Description: Wingspan 51–65mm (2–2½ in). Uppersides are a rich tawny orange-brown with darker bars and patches and a series of yellow spots on the outer half of the forewing. Hindwings have a row of black spots with orange haloes near the rear margin. Undersides are whitish with violet-brown areas, black markings and black spots with blue centres on the hindwings.
Life Cycle: Pale green eggs are laid in batches of 200–500 on leaves and the caterpillars remain together for much of their lives. They are sluglike, green with yellow and white stripes, two short tails at the rear end and two branched spines on the head. The pale green pupa also has two horns at the head end. Larvae overwinter in shelters made from leaves webbed to branches. In the extreme south of the range the butterflies are about for much of the year, but further north only June–September.

Larval Foodplants: Hackberries (*Celtis* species).
General Remarks: Tawny Emperors are locally common in the south of their range, rarer in the north. They love to feed on overripe fruit, and are also seen on tree sap and carrion, but rarely on flowers.

TAWNY EMPEROR

Asterocampa clyton

HACKBERRY BUTTERFLY

Asterocampa celtis

Family: Nymphalidae.

Habitat: Wooded areas, also city suburbs and parks.

Distribution: Central and eastern states of U.S.A., Mexico.

Description: Wingspan 41–57mm ($1\frac{3}{4}$–$2\frac{1}{4}$ in). Uppersides are varying shades of brown, ranging from grey-brown to orange-brown, with darker forewing tips, on which there are white and cream blotches, and dark wavy lines and spots on hindwings. Wings have green sheen when fresh. Undersides are much paler with series of dark spots with paler centres and haloes.

Life Cycle: Eggs are pale green or cream, usually laid singly on new growth. Caterpillars are green and slug-shaped, with yellow lines, two pointed tails at rear, and two small branched horns on the head. They hibernate as caterpillars. Several broods of the butterflies in south Texas and Florida fly March to November; further north usually two broods, seen June–September.

Larval Foodplants: Hackberries (*Celtis* species).

General Remarks: Hackberry Butterflies feed on fruit, sap, and sometimes on flower nectar, carrion and dung. Males find perches on which to await females, choosing an elevated spot. This is often a small tree or tree trunk in a sunny position, but they will often land on a person's head instead. The planting of hackberries as ornamentals in cities and suburbs has enabled this butterfly to establish and spread there, perching on buildings and patrolling along blocks, flying well into dusk.

Family: Nymphalidae.

Habitat: Forest margins, fields, scrub, and suburbs of towns.

Distribution: In U.S.A. commonest in southern States, but migrates northwards, sometimes reaching Canada. Southwards, the range extends to Argentina.

Description: Wingspan 64–73mm ($2\frac{1}{2}$–$2\frac{7}{8}$ in). Uppersides are bright red-orange. The long, narrow forewings have black streaks and a group of black-rimmed white spots near the upper margin; hindwings have a network of black on rear margins. Undersides are even lovelier, with a pink basal area on the forewing and beautiful elongated spots of metallic silver on the hindwing and forewing tip.

Life Cycle: Yellow eggs are laid singly on the leaves, stems and tendrils of the foodplant. The caterpillars are greyish-black, with cream dots, reddish lines, six rows of long black branching spines on the body, plus two backward-curving spines on the head. In southern parts of Florida, Texas and California there are several broods of butterflies, flying throughout the year, but further north they are only seen in the summer and cannot survive the winter.

Larval Foodplants: Passion flowers (*Passiflora* species).

General Remarks: Gulf Fritillaries migrate northwards in spring and early summer, and there are return southerly flights in late summer and autumn. They fly very rapidly, usually within a few metres of the ground. They are often seen feeding on flowers, particularly red and white ones.

GULF FRITILLARY

Dione (Agraulis) vanillae

GREAT SPANGLED FRITILLARY

Speyeria cybele

Family: Nymphalidae.

Habitat: Moist woods and meadows, marshes, open spaces and roadsides.

Distribution: Southern Canada and northern U.S.A. south to central California, New Mexico and north Georgia.

Description: Wingspan 54–76mm ($2\frac{1}{8}$–3 in). Uppersides are tawny orange with patterning of black streaks and spots. Undersides have areas of reddish-brown and yellowish-orange with silver spots and a border of silver triangles on the hindwing.

Life Cycle: Eggs are pale yellow, becoming tan, and are laid singly near the foodplants. The larvae seek hibernation sites soon after hatching, before they have fed. They become active again in spring, feeding on leaves at night. The full-grown caterpillars are velvety black, with lines of grey dots and many orange spines with black tips. They pupate in late spring, producing butterflies which fly from June to September in most areas.

Larval Foodplants: Violets (*Viola* species).

General Remarks: Great Spangled Fritillaries are commonest in the eastern part of their range, occurring widely in the Atlantic states. They fly very rapidly, but are very attracted to flowers and may be seen drinking nectar from Black-eyed Susans, thistles and others. Occasionally they feed on dung.

This species is one of a group of medium to large Fritillary butterflies which have a broadly similar appearance of tawny-orange and black uppersides and attractive silver spotting on the undersides. Suitable habitats with violets are usually a critical requirement.

Family: Nymphalidae.

Habitat: Wet meadows and bogs, sometimes clearings in woods.

Distribution: Most of Canada except far north, and into Alaska; only the extreme north of the U.S.A., except in the Rockies where range extends south to northern New Mexico. Europe, including Britain, and central Asia.

Description: Wingspan 35–51mm (1⅜–2 in). Uppersides are tawny-orange to ochreous with black spots and streaks and black zig-zag line near outer margins. Undersides are an attractive mosaic of pale yellow, red-

brown and, on the hindwing, silver, with black outlines. There is a border of triangular silver spots to the hindwing underside.

Life Cycle: Pale green eggs are usually laid near to foodplants, rather than on them. The caterpillars hibernate when fairly small and resume feeding in spring. When full-grown they are dark grey-black, mottled with yellow, and with many orangish cones with spines, and two long projections behind the head. There are two or three flights of butterflies in the May–September period over much of its North American range, but only one brood in June–August in the Rockies and far north, also usually only one in Britain, in June.

Larval Foodplants: Violets (*Viola* species).

General Remarks: This butterfly may be seen feeding on flowers such as Red Clover (*Trifolium pratense*) and Vervain (*Verbena hastata*) in North America and Bugle (*Ajuga reptans*) in Britain. Commonest on eastern side of North America, but western side of Britain.

SILVER-BORDERED FRITILLARY (U.S.A.); SMALL PEARL-BORDERED FRITILLARY (U.K.)

Boloria selene

VICEROY

Limenitis archippus

Family: Nymphalidae.

Habitat: Near water and in woods, also open meadows and roadsides.

Distribution: Most of eastern and central North America south of Hudson Bay, and into Mexico.

Description: Quite large, wingspan 67–76mm ($2\frac{5}{8}$–3 in). Wings are the same colour on upper and undersides, varying from deep chestnut in the south to pale tawny orange in the north. On this background are black veins, black borders with white spots, and a black area with white blotches on the forewing. The hindwing usually has a black line curving across it.

Life Cycle: Pale yellow-green eggs are laid singly on leaf tips. Caterpillars feed on catkins, then leaves, mainly at night. Full-grown caterpillars are brown or olive with a cream or pinkish saddle-shaped patch on the back and two feathery black horns behind the head. Both the caterpillar and chrysalis mimic bird droppings. Caterpillars hibernate in leaf shelters. There are four generations of butterflies in the south, flying from spring to autumn, but only one or two broods further north, flying in the June–August period.

Larval Foodplants: Willows (*Salix*), also poplars and aspens (*Populus*), and sometimes plum (*Prunus*) and apple (*Malus*).

General Remarks: Viceroys feed on flowers, aphid honeydew and tree sap. They mimic the appearance of the distasteful Monarch butterfly in the north and the Queen butterfly in the south, thus gaining protection by fooling predators.

Family: Danaidae
Habitat: Meadows, weedy fields and watercourses with milkweeds, but may be seen almost anywhere when migrating.
Distribution: Throughout North America up as far as Hudson Bay, Central and South America, Australasia. Very occasionally blown across the Atlantic to Britain.
Description: Large, wingspan 89–102mm ($3\frac{1}{2}$–4 in). Bright burnt-orange with black veins, black margins sprinkled with white dots, and white and orange spots in black forewing tip. Undersides are much paler orange.

Life Cycle: Eggs are pale green and caterpillars very striking, with alternating black, yellow and white bands around the body, and a pair of long black filaments behind the head. Chrysalis is pale green, studded with gold points. Flight period of butterflies varies with latitude, starting in spring in southern U.S.A., but not seen until summer further north.
Larval Foodplants: Milkweeds (*Asclepias*) and Dogbane (*Apocynum*).
General Remarks: Probably the world's best known butterfly, the Monarch is famed for its tremendous migrations throughout the length of North America, and the spectacular congregations of butterflies at their overwintering roosts on trees in California and central Mexico, now tourist attractions.

Monarch caterpillars accumulate heart poisons from the milkweeds on which they feed and pass them on to the butterflies. Most birds soon learn not to eat them.

MONARCH

Danaus plexippus

RINGLET (U.S.A.);
LARGE HEATH (U.K.)

Coenonympha tullia

Family: Satyridae.

Habitat: Foothills, grassy glades in pine forests, arctic tundra and mountain canyons in the U.S.A., boggy places and damp moors in the U.K.

Distribution: Much of Canada and into Alaska, north-western U.S.A. and into California. Europe, including northern parts of Britain, and temperate Asia.

Description: Wingspan 36–41mm ($1\frac{3}{8}$–$1\frac{5}{8}$ in). Undersides are various shades of grey, with eyespots that vary in number and intensity between butterflies from different localities. Uppersides are rarely seen because the butterflies always rest with wings closed. In North America they vary in colour from orange-brown in the east to cream in California and Alaska. In Britain they are grey-brown.

Life Cycle: Eggs are pale yellow-green and caterpillars hibernate when small. Full-grown caterpillars are green with tiny white hairs, a dark green stripe along the back, white stripes on the sides and two short pinkish tails at the rear. The number of generations of butterflies, and their flight period, varies with latitude, ranging from several broods flying May–September in parts of western U.S.A., to one brood in June–July in the far north, high Rockies, and in Britain.

Larval Foodplants: Various grasses, such as species of *Poa*, also Cotton Grass (*Eriophorum*) and other sedges in Europe.

General Remarks: The Large Heath has a weak, fluttering flight close to the ground, so it is inconspicuous. It usually lives in discrete colonies.

Family: Satyridae.
Habitat: Moist grassy places and open woodland.
Distribution: Most of the U.S.A. except the south-west, and into Canada.
Description: Wingspan 52–73mm (2–3 in). It is very variable in colour and markings. Uppersides range from light to dark brown, usually with two eyespots on each forewing. Eyespots are sometimes large, with white or blue centres, and may be surrounded by a yellow area. Undersides have a marbled brown pattern with several eyespots.

Life Cycle: Pale lemon eggs are laid on or near foodplants. A female may lay 200–300 eggs. The caterpillar is green, with a darker line on the back, yellow stripes down the sides, and two reddish tails. There is one flight of butterflies, usually from late June to early September and their eggs produce larvae that go into hibernation without feeding.
Larval Foodplants: Various grasses such as *Andropogon* and *Tridens flavus*.
General Remarks: Wood Nymph butterflies feed on the nectar of flowers such as Alfalfa (*Medicago sativa*) and *Spiraea*, and occasionally on sap, rotting fruit or dung. They also perch on tree trunks, where they blend beautifully with the bark.

Males patrol throughout the day in grassy areas to look for females. After a chase a male will land near the female and waft his pheromone (sex attractant scent) over her by a rapid fluttering of his wings, thus stimulating her to mate.

WOOD NYMPH

Cercyonis pegala

SPECKLED WOOD

Pararge aegeria

Family: Satyridae.
Habitat: Woodland fringes and clearings, lanes and hedgerows.
Distribution: Most of Britain except parts of northern England and Scotland. Also, much of continental Europe, North Africa and parts of Asia.
Description: Wingspan 32–45mm ($1\frac{1}{4}$–$1\frac{3}{4}$ in). Uppersides of wings have an attractive pattern of creamy-yellow patches on a dark brown background, with three black spots with white centres on the hindwing and one near the tip of the forewing. This spot can also be seen on the grey and brown undersides.
Life Cycle: Eggs are pale yellow and caterpillars pale green, with faint white and yellow lines and a pair of short white protruberances at the rear. This species can overwinter either as a caterpillar or a chrysalis. In southern England there may be as many as three broods of butterflies, flying between April and September, with fewer broods in the north.
Larval Foodplants: Grasses such as Cocksfoot (*Dactylis glomerata*) and Couch (*Agropyron repens*).
General Remarks: Speckled Woods are often seen in semi-shade, where their coloration blends beautifully with the dappled sunshine on the leaves. Males perch for long periods, leaving only to chase females or drive away other males. Butterflies feed on aphid honeydew, and sometimes bramble blossom. Numbers have been increasing in Britain over the last half-century, and the range has expanded.

Family: Satyridae.

Habitat: Woodland edges and clearings, scrubby areas, hedgerows and lanes.

Distribution: Southern and central England, Wales, extreme south of Ireland, and much of continental Europe.

Description: Wingspan 40–47mm ($1\frac{1}{2}$–$1\frac{7}{8}$ in). Much of the wing is a bright orange, with grey-brown borders and a black spot containing two white dots near the forewing tip. Males have a dark band dividing the

orange area on the forewing and are smaller than females. Hindwing undersides are mottled brown with white dots, forewing dull brown with the black spot with two white dots.

Life Cycle: Pale, ridged eggs are laid singly and caterpillars hibernate when small, resuming feeding in May and producing butterflies in July–August. Full-grown caterpillars are fawn or grey with dark lines and short white hairs.

Larval Foodplants: Grasses, including bents (*Agrostis* species), fescues (*Festuca*), meadow grasses (*Poa*) and Couch (*Agropyron repens*).

General Remarks: Gatekeepers are fairly common in suitable habitats in southern England, becoming rarer to the north. They have a jerky, fairly rapid, flight and may be seen feeding on flowers, particularly brambles and yellow ones, or basking on the leaves of shrubs or hedges.

The so-called Satyr butterflies in this family usually have wings in shades of brown or orange, often with eyespots. The spindle-shaped caterpillars feed on various grasses and grow rather slowly.

GATEKEEPER OR HEDGE BROWN

Pyronia tithonus

SPRING AZURE (U.S.A.); HOLLY BLUE (U.K.)

Celastrina argiolus

Family: Lycaenidae.

Habitat: Open woodland, hedgerows, also parks and gardens.

Distribution: Most of North America, including Canada and Alaska to the edge of the tundra; Central America. Europe, including southern half of Britain, also North Africa and Asia.

Description: Small, wingspan 20–32mm ($\frac{3}{4}$–$1\frac{1}{4}$ in). It has many subspecies and forms which differ slightly in appearance. Males are usually a lovely lilac blue, females similar but with a wide black border to the forewing. Females sometimes have white replacing blue in the U.S.A.. Undersides are silver grey, usually with black dots, sometimes more extensive dark dashes and zigzags.

Life Cycle: Pale green eggs are laid singly on flower buds, caterpillars eating flowers and berries. Caterpillars are usually green, sometimes with pink or brown shading. It hibernates as a pupa. In Canada there is usually one flight of butterflies, May–June or later, but in most of the U.S.A. there are several flights between March and September. Two broods in Britain, flying April–May and July–August.

Larval Foodplants: Unusual, in that caterpillars from different generations feed on different plants. Many hosts in North America, especially dogwoods (*Cornus*), *Viburnum*, *Ceanothus* and blueberries (*Vaccinium*). In Britain, Holly (*Ilex*) (first brood) and Ivy (*Hedera*) (second) are mainly used.

General Remarks: One of the first butterflies to be seen in spring in North America. Seldom seen on flowers, but flies around shrubs and perches on leaves with wings half open.

Family: Lycaenidae.
Habitat: Grassland on chalk and limestone hills, cliffs, dunes, heaths and abandoned quarries, waste ground.
Distribution: Ranges from North Africa to the Arctic, including Britain and the rest of Europe.
Description: Quite a small butterfly, wingspan averaging 35mm ($1\frac{3}{8}$ in). Males are a lovely bright blue, with

white fringes to the wings. Females vary in colour, ranging from brown with only a small area of blue near the body to a form in which a large proportion of the wings is a vivid violet-blue. All females have a series of orange crescents and black spots on the outer margins. Male undersides are grey, females brown. Both have white spots with black centres, and orange crescents near the margins.
Life Cycle: White, disc-shaped eggs are laid singly on young terminal leaves. Caterpillars are green. In southern England two broods of butterflies fly in May–June and late July–September: further north there is one generation in July–August. Late summer caterpillars hibernate.
Larval Foodplants: Mainly Bird's-foot Trefoil (*Lotus corniculatus*), but sometimes Restharrows (*Ononis* species), Black Medick (*Medicago lupulina*) and Clovers (*Trifolium*).
General Remarks: As its name implies, this species is the commonest blue butterfly in Britain, sometimes even occurring on the fringes of towns. It usually lives in discrete colonies.

COMMON BLUE

Polyommatus icarus

CHALKHILL BLUE

Lysandra coridon

Family: Lycaenidae.

Habitat: Short grassland on chalk and limestone.

Distribution: Southern England and throughout most of Europe.

Description: One of the largest of European blue butterflies, wingspan around 38mm ($1\frac{1}{2}$ in). Males are a distinctive silvery-blue, with a black border, of variable width, to the forewing. In flight, they appear paler than other blue butterflies. In contrast, females are sooty-brown with black spots, edged with white and orange, on outer margin of hindwing. Male undersides are light grey, females brownish, both with variable number of spots.

Life Cycle: One generation of butterflies flies in July–August. Females lay disc-shaped eggs on vegetation: these do not hatch until following spring. Woodlouse-shaped caterpillars are green with yellow broken stripes.

Larval Foodplants: Mainly Horseshoe Vetch (*Hippocrepis comosa*), occasionally Bird's-foot Trefoil (*Lotus corniculatus*) or Kidney Vetch (*Anthyllis vulneraria*).

General Remarks: Chalkhill Blues have disappeared from many former sites in England as downland has been ploughed up, or because lack of grazing by sheep or rabbits has resulted in the foodplants becoming overgrown. They live in compact colonies.

Like the caterpillars of many other blue butterflies, those of the Chalkhill Blue are attended by ants. The ants are attracted by a sugary solution exuded from a special gland on the caterpillar's body, and in return for this food they may protect the larvae from predators and parasites.

Family: Lycaenidae.
Habitat: Meadows and fields, forest clearings, gardens, and disturbed sites such as roadsides.
Distribution: U.S.A. east of the Rockies, south-east Canada, also California and Mexico.
Description: Small, wingspan 20–25mm ($\frac{3}{4}$–1 in). Males are a beautiful bright blue on the upperside, with thin black borders and white fringes. Females are mainly brown, though

with some blue, more obvious in the spring brood. Both have a slender tail on the rear of each hindwing, with two orange spots with black centres nearby, visible on both sides of the wing. The rest of the undersides is greyish-white with curved rows of grey-black spots.
Life Cycle: Pale green eggs are laid singly, usually on flowers. Caterpillars eat flowers or leaves. They are usually dark green with many pale dots, a dark green stripe on the back, and whitish lines on the sides, and hibernate when almost fully grown. There are several generations of butterflies during the year, flying February–November on the Gulf Coast and May–October in the north.
Larval Foodplants: Leguminous plants such as tick trefoils (*Desmodium*), bush clovers (*Lespedeza*), clovers (*Trifolium*), Everlasting Pea (*Lathyrus*), and beans (*Phaseolus*).
General Remarks: One of the commonest butterflies in eastern U.S.A. Visits flowers and mud puddles. A very similar species, the Western Tailed Blue, flies in western areas and in places the two occur together.

EASTERN TAILED BLUE

Everes comyntas

GREAT PURPLE OR GREAT BLUE HAIRSTREAK

Atlides halesus

Family: Lycaenidae.

Habitat: Wooded areas, particularly clearings near trees infested with mistletoe.

Distribution: Most of U.S.A. south of latitude 38°, and extends further north in coastal areas to New York in the east and northern Oregon in the west.

Description: Quite small, wingspan 32–38mm ($1\frac{1}{4}$–$1\frac{1}{2}$ in). Male has beautiful iridescent metallic blue uppersides, with black margins and a black spot on the hindwing. Female has smaller area of blue. Both sexes have two long, thin tails on the hindwing. Undersides are mainly brown, with red spots near the red body.

Life Cycle: Caterpillars are green with yellow stripes on the sides and a darker green line on the back, and feed on leaves and flowers. They pupate at the base of a tree or under loose bark and the chrysalis overwinters. In many areas there are two broods of butterflies, in February–April and, usually in higher numbers, in July–October.

Larval Foodplants: Mistletoe (*Phoradendron flavescens*) on various trees such as poplars (*Populus*), walnut (*Juglans*) and ash (*Fraxinus*).

General Remarks: One of the most brilliantly coloured North American butterflies, its wings changing colour as they change angle to the light. As on other Hairstreak butterflies, the tails look like antennae when the wings are closed, and eye-like markings near the base of the tails make up a false head which distracts birds from the real one.

Family: Lycaenidae.
Habitat: Meadows, roadsides, waste places and hillsides, also mountain areas.
Distribution: Much of north-eastern U.S.A. and eastern Canada, also parts of the Rockies, central California, British Columbia and Alaska. Occurs into the Arctic. Throughout Europe including Britain, across temperate Asia to Japan; North Africa.
Description: Small, wingspan 25–35mm ($1-1\frac{3}{8}$ in). Uppersides of fore-wings are a lovely coppery orange

with black spots and margins; hindwings are black with orange margins, with a line of blue spots on some specimens. Undersides are dull orange and grey.
Life Cycle: Eggs are like small white golf balls. Caterpillars are green or dull pink and slug-like. There is one brood of butterflies in northern regions flying June–September, but further south there may be several broods, so they may be seen for much of the period from April to October.
Larval Foodplants: Sorrels and docks (*Rumex* species and *Oxyria digyna*).
General Remarks: This is now the only species of Copper butterfly to occur naturally in Britain, but there are several species in North America and continental Europe, usually with lovely burnished copper or purple colouring.

Within this species there is much variation in markings between individuals and seasons. The butterflies only move very short distances and are usually seen only in ones or twos. Despite their small size they are quite pugnacious, chasing away other butterflies from their territories.

AMERICAN OR FLAME COPPER (U.S.A.); SMALL COPPER (U.K.)

Lycaena phlaeas

ORANGE TIP

Anthocharis cardamines

Family: Pieridae.

Habitat: Hedgerows, damp meadows, woodland clearings and along riverbanks.

Distribution: Most of Europe and eastwards across temperate Asia to China and Japan.

Description: Wingspan 45–50mm ($1\frac{3}{4}$–2 in). Upperside of wings white, with bright orange tips to forewings in the male, dark grey tips in the female. Both sexes have a marbled greenish pattern on the undersides of the wings, providing superb camouflage when at rest on vegetation.

Life Cycle: Adults fly late April and May. Orange eggs are laid, usually singly, on the flower stalks of the foodplants. Caterpillars are bluish-green above, dark green below, with white band along sides. They feed on seedpods in June and early July (and sometimes on each other!). A characteristic triangular-shaped chrysalis is the overwintering stage.

Larval Foodplants: Garlic Mustard (*Alliaria petiolata*), Lady's Smock (*Cardamine pratensis*), Hedge Mustard (*Sisymbrium officinale*), and some related cruciferous plants. In gardens, Honesty (*Lunaria annua*), Dame's Violet (*Hesperis matronalis*) and *Arabis*.

General Remarks: Has been extending its range in Britain into northern England and southern Scotland since the 1970s. However, local extinctions have occurred where hedgerows have been removed, meadows drained, or verges sprayed with herbicide.

Very similar species occur in North America, including the Sara Orange Tip in western U.S.A. and Falcate Orange Tip and Olympia Marble in central and eastern U.S.A. Their caterpillars also feed on plants of the mustard family, Cruciferae.

Family: Pieridae.
Habitat: Clearings, prairie, foothill chaparral, open woodlands.
Distribution: Central United States and into southern central Canada, where it is expanding its range.
Description: Wingspan 38–44mm ($1\frac{1}{2}$–$1\frac{3}{4}$ in). Wings are white, with yellow-green marbling on the underside of the hindwings which shows through to the uppersides. There are

grey marks near the tip of the forewing. In certain locations some have a rosy pink flush on the basal part of the hindwing.

Life Cycle: Eggs are orange, laid singly on unopened flower buds. Young caterpillars eat flowers and seeds, older ones eat leaves also. Caterpillars are green on the back, with grey and yellow stripes along the sides. This species hibernates as a grey-brown pupa. The butterflies emerge in spring, flying mid-April–mid-May in southern parts of their range, and late April–early June in parts of Canada and the Colorado foothills.

Larval Foodplants: Cruciferous plants such as Rock Cress (*Arabis* species) and Hedge Mustard (*Sisymbrium officinale*).

General Remarks: Olympia Marbles are rather uncommon in general, but can be numerous locally, particularly in the Mid-West. Their numbers fluctuate dramatically from year to year. There are several species of Marble Butterflies in North America with a similar appearance to the Olympia, and they are closely related to the Orange Tips.

OLYMPIA OR ROSY MARBLE

Euchloe olympia

SMALL OR CABBAGE WHITE

Pieris (Artogeia) rapae

Family: Pieridae.

Habitat: May be seen almost anywhere, but particularly around gardens and fields with brassica crops.

Distribution: Europe, including Britain, and across Siberia to Japan. Accidently introduced to Quebec in 1860, and has spread throughout North America, from Hudson Bay to southern Mexico.

Description: Wingspan 38–51mm (1½–2 in). Uppersides are white with dark grey tips to the forewings, which also have one black spot in the male, two in the female. Spring broods have fainter markings than summer butterflies. The undersides of the hindwings and forewing tips are lemon yellow, dusted with grey.

Life Cycle: Pale yellow, bottle-shaped eggs are laid singly, but often several to a plant. One female may lay as many as 700 eggs. Caterpillars are bluish-green with a yellowish line down the back and yellow spots on the sides. They feed on leaves and bore into the hearts of cabbages. In southern U.S.A. and Europe there are many generations of butterflies flying from early spring to autumn, while further north there are fewer broods over a shorter period.

Larval Foodplants: Cabbages and related brassica crops, wild crucifers, Nasturtium (*Tropaeolum*), and mignonettes (*Reseda*).

General Remarks: It has become one of the most successful butterfly colonisers and a very serious pest of brassicas, particularly before the advent of more effective insecticides. Tiny wasps that parasitize the caterpillars have also been used.

Family: Pieridae.

Habitat: Streamsides, damp meadows and ditches, but mainly forest clearings and woodland in the U.S.A.

Distribution: Much of Canada and into Alaska, some western parts of U.S.A., Europe, including Britain, and Asia.

Description: Wingspan 38–50mm ($1\frac{1}{2}$–2 in). The grey-green edging to the veins of the yellowish undersides of the wings distinguishes it from other white butterflies. This vein-marking may be fainter on summer

broods of the butterfly. Uppersides are white with dark tips and sometimes dark spots on the forewings. Sometimes veins appear dark on the uppersides also.

Life Cycle: Pale yellow eggs are laid singly on leaves or stems. Caterpillars are green with black dots, a darker green stripe on the back, and yellowish stripes or dots on the sides. It hibernates as a pupa. In northern Canada and much of the Rockies there is one flight of butterflies in June–July, elsewhere in North America two or three flights in the April–August period. Similarly, in southern Britain there are two or occasionally three broods in April–September, but only one in June–July in northern Scotland.

Larval Foodplants: Cruciferous plants such as cresses (species of *Arabis*, *Barbarea* and *Thlaspi*), mustards (*Sisymbrium*), *Brassica* and *Cardamine* species, and toothworts (*Dentaria*).

General Remarks: A common and widely distributed butterfly in Britain, but in eastern North America its range has decreased due to deforestation.

SHARP-VEINED OR MUSTARD WHITE (U.S.A.); GREEN-VEINED WHITE (U.K.)

Pieris (Artogeia) napi

ORANGE SULPHUR or ALFALFA BUTTERFLY

Colias eurytheme

Family: Pieridae.

Habitat: Open areas at all altitudes, Alfalfa fields.

Distribution: Throughout the United States, to southern Mexico, and, more rarely, into southern Canada.

Description: Wingspan 41–60mm ($1\frac{5}{8}$–$2\frac{3}{8}$ in). Uppersides are usually bright orange with black borders, though in spring they may be yellow with an orange flush, and some females are white. Undersides are orange, with a single or double red-rimmed silvery spot on the hindwing. Wings have a pink fringe.

Life Cycle: Long, creamy-white eggs are laid singly on leaves. A single female may lay as many as 700. Caterpillars are dark green, sometimes with white or pink stripes on the sides. There are many generations of butterflies, flying March–December in the south, but over a shorter period in the north.

Larval Foodplants: Chiefly Alfalfa (*Medicago sativa*), but also other leguminous plants such as White Clover (*Trifolium repens*), Milk Vetch (*Astragalus*) and lupins (*Lupinus*).

General Remarks: Orange Sulphurs are widespread and sometimes abundant over much of their range, except the northern and southern extremes. Their caterpillars are sometimes a pest in Alfalfa fields.

This species is often seen in large numbers in association with the closely-related Common Sulphur, which is yellow rather than orange. Their strong flight, and the wide food range of their larvae, enable these two butterflies to colonise disturbed and cultivated areas rapidly.

Family: Pieridae.
Habitat: Open woodlands, oak scrub and deserts, but straying to other areas.
Distribution: Southern areas of United States and south to Argentina. Also stray northwards into California, northern States, and occasionally southern Canada.
Description: Wingspan 45–64mm ($1\frac{3}{4}$–$2\frac{1}{2}$ in). It can be recognized by the distinctive poodle's-head shape in the outline of the black border to the yellow forewings, which have a pointed tip. Hindwings are yellow with a thin black edge. Females are sometimes white. Undersides are yellow with reddish-pink mottling.
Life Cycle: Eggs are yellow-green, turning to crimson, and are laid singly on terminal leaves of the foodplants. Caterpillars are very variable in appearance, but are often yellow-green with many black points, and yellowish-white bands and orange dashes down the sides. The butterflies fly throughout the year in southern parts of Texas and Florida, but further north there are fewer generations and a shorter flight period in mid to late summer.

Larval Foodplants: Leguminous plants such as False Indigo and Lead Plant (*Amorpha* species), and clovers (*Trifolium* species).
General Remarks: Like many other species of *Colias*, Dog Face butterflies are migrants, moving north from their base in the southern States, where they are quite common. They have a very rapid flight, but may be seen feeding on flowers or drinking at mud.

DOG FACE

Colias (Zerene) cesonia

BRIMSTONE

Gonepteryx rhamni

Family: Pieridae.

Habitat: Woodlands, but straying into open countryside and gardens.

Distribution: Throughout Europe except northern Scandinavia. In Britain it is commonest in southern areas and very rare in Scotland.

Description: Quite large, wingspan around 60mm (2½ in). Males are a bright sulphur yellow, females a paler greenish lemon, both with an orange spot on each wing. The leaf-shaped outline of the wings when closed provides excellent camouflage when resting in vegetation.

Life Cycle: Brimstones overwinter as adults and are among the first butterflies to be seen on warm days in spring. The bluish-green caterpillars feed in early summer, producing the next generation of butterflies in August. These will feed until October or November, then hibernate. Some Brimstones may live for 11 months, making them among the longest-lived of butterflies.

Larval Foodplants: Common Buckthorn (*Rhamnus cartharticus*) and Alder Buckthorn (*Frangula alnus*).

General Remarks: It is thought that the Brimstone may have given rise to the term 'butterfly', through a contraction of 'butter-coloured fly'.

The tubular tongue (proboscis) of Brimstones is long (17mm, 0.67in), enabling them to feed on flowers whose nectar is concealed at the end of a long tube. In spring they feed on flowers such as dandelions (*Taraxacum officinale*), Primroses (*Primula vulgaris*), Bluebells (*Endymion nonscriptus*) and Bugle (*Ajuga reptans*), while in late summer they often choose knapweeds (*Centaurea* species) and teasels (*Dipsacus fullonum*).

Family: Libytheidae.
Habitat: Woodland and thorn forest, near streams.
Distribution: Much of U.S.A., but most numerous in south-eastern States. Ranges south to northern South America.
Description: Wingspan 41–48mm ($1\frac{5}{8}$–$1\frac{7}{8}$ in). Uppersides are dark brown with orange patches and large white spots, of variable size. Forewings have squared-off tips. Undersides are a duller version of the uppersides.

Life Cycle: Pale green eggs are laid singly on young leaves. Caterpillars are usually dark green above, yellowish-green below, with many yellow points and black tubercles on a hump behind the head. Several broods of butterflies fly throughout the year in southern Texas and Florida, but with a shorter flight period further north. They hibernate as adults in the south.
Larval Foodplants: Hackberries (*Celtis* species).
General Remarks: Snout butterflies are strong migrants, sometimes moving northward in large swarms and spreading from the south to central and northern areas, sometimes reaching Ontario, North Dakota, Maine and California. In some years they may be common in the northern U.S.A. in late summer. The butterflies are often seen on mud, also on flowers and fruit.

The characteristic long palpi (mouthparts) on the head of this butterfly form the 'snout' which gives it its common name. When the butterfly is resting on a twig, the palpi resemble a leaf stalk and the closed wings the leaf, so camouflaging it from predators.

SNOUT

Libytheana carinenta

EUROPEAN SKIPPER (U.S.A.); ESSEX SKIPPER (U.K.)

Thymelicus lineola

Family: Hesperiidae.
Habitat: Meadows, rough grassland, hayfields.
Distribution: Europe, including southern England, and east to Asia, also North Africa. North-east U.S.A., south-east Canada and British Columbia.
Description: Small, wingspan 19–31mm ($\frac{3}{4}$–$1\frac{1}{4}$ in). Uppersides are bright orange-brown with faint black veins and black margins. Undersides are dull orange-brown, tinged with grey-green.
Life Cycle: Whitish eggs are laid in rows on grass stems. Caterpillars are pale green, with a darker stripe down the back and yellow lines on the sides. They live and feed April–June in a tube made from a grass blade held together by silk. The green chrysalis is also formed in a silk tent between blades of grass. Butterflies fly in June–July or July–August, depending on latitude, and produce eggs that overwinter.
Larval Foodplants: Grasses such as Timothy (*Phleum pratense*) and Cocksfoot (*Dactylis glomerata*).
General Remarks: This species was introduced into Ontario from Europe in 1910, and since then it has spread about 25km per year, so that it now occupies a large part of eastern North America. Another introduction occurred in British Columbia in 1960, and it is now established there. Caterpillars of this butterfly are now an important pest on hay crops in some parts of North America.

Skipper butterflies have short, stumpy wings, usually held half open, with fore and hindwings apart.